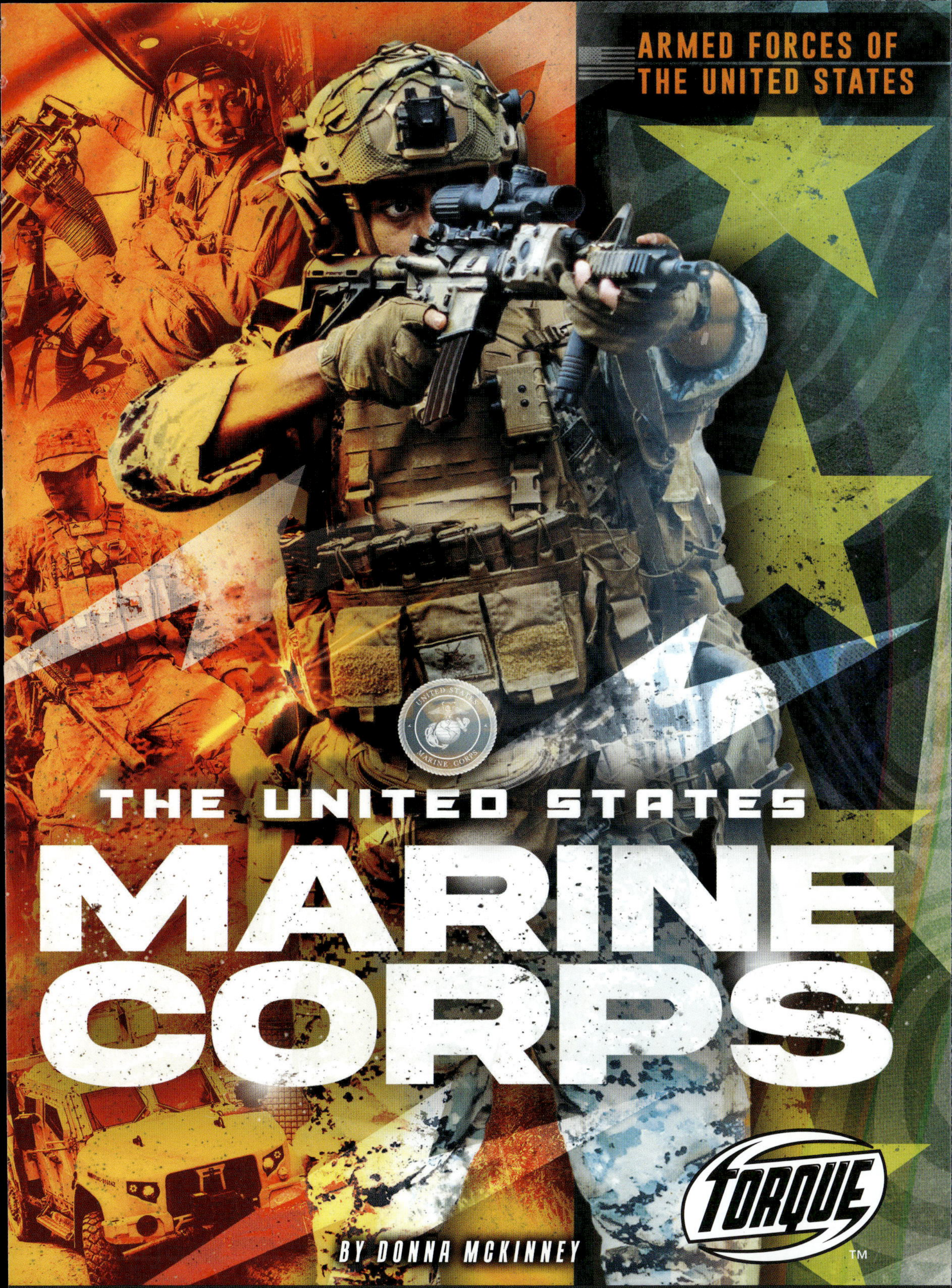

ARMED FORCES OF THE UNITED STATES

THE UNITED STATES MARINE CORPS

BY DONNA MCKINNEY

TORQUE™

BELLWETHER MEDIA • MINNEAPOLIS, MN

Torque brims with excitement perfect for thrill-seekers of all kinds. Discover daring survival skills, explore uncharted worlds, and marvel at mighty engines and extreme sports. In *Torque* books, anything can happen. Are you ready?

This edition first published in 2025 by Bellwether Media, Inc.

Library of Congress Cataloging-in-Publication Data

Names: McKinney, Donna B. (Donna Bowen) author.
Title: The United States Marine Corps / by Donna McKinney.
Description: Minneapolis, MN : Bellwether Media, Inc., 2025. |
Series: Armed forces of the United States | Includes bibliographical references and index. | Audience: Ages 7-12 | Audience: Grades 4-6 |
Summary: "Engaging images accompany information about the United States Marine Corps. The combination of high-interest subject matter and light text is intended for students in grades 3 through 7"– Provided by publisher.
Identifiers: LCCN 2024016019 (print) | LCCN 2024016020 (ebook) | ISBN 9798893040135 (library binding) | ISBN 9781644879450 (ebook)
Subjects: LCSH: United States. Marine Corps–Juvenile literature. | Marines–United States–Juvenile literature.
Classification: LCC VE23 .M3934 2025 (print) | LCC VE23 (ebook) | DDC 359.9/60973–dc23/eng/20240411
LC record available at https://lccn.loc.gov/2024016019
LC ebook record available at https://lccn.loc.gov/2024016020

Editor: Rebecca Sabelko Designer: Jeffrey Kollock

Printed in the United States of America, North Mankato, MN.

TABLE OF CONTENTS

EARTHQUAKE! 4
ALWAYS READY 6
MARINES WEAPONS, VEHICLES, AND AIRCRAFT 10
MISSIONS 14
MARINE CORPS PROFILE 20
GLOSSARY 22
TO LEARN MORE 23
INDEX 24

EARTHQUAKE!

It is April 2016. **Earthquakes** have hit Japan. Many people on the island of Kyushu need help. The United States Marine Corps is ready to give aid.

Marines bring supplies to the island. They carry food and shelter kits. But **landslides** keep rescuers from reaching a mountain village. Marines fly MV-22 Ospreys and other aircraft. They get supplies to the village.

ALWAYS READY

The Marine Corps conducts **missions** around the world. Members are called Marines. They are part of the Department of the Navy. Some Marines serve on Navy ships. Others work at **bases** on land.

The **Pentagon** is the Marine Corps **headquarters**. Marine bases are in the U.S. and Japan. Marines also work at U.S. **embassies** in other countries.

MARINES

PENTAGON

MARINES AT U.S. EMBASSY IN CANBERRA, AUSTRALIA

Marines are often the first troops to act during wars. They use aircraft and **armored combat vehicles**. They also use weapons.

CODE TALKERS

Twenty-nine Navajo men helped the Marines send secret messages during World War II. They were called Code Talkers. They were important to U.S. success in World War II.

Marines train for war during times of peace. They carry out peacekeeping missions in other countries. They keep U.S. embassies safe. They also help when **natural disasters** strike.

MARINE CORPS BASES

MARINES WEAPONS, VEHICLES, AND AIRCRAFT

Marines have different weapons. They carry guns like M27 Infantry Automatic Rifles. These guns are light and easy to handle. They use M203 Grenade Launchers. These single-shot weapons are often fixed to guns.

AMPHIBIOUS COMBAT VEHICLE

NUMBER IN USE AT LEAST 139

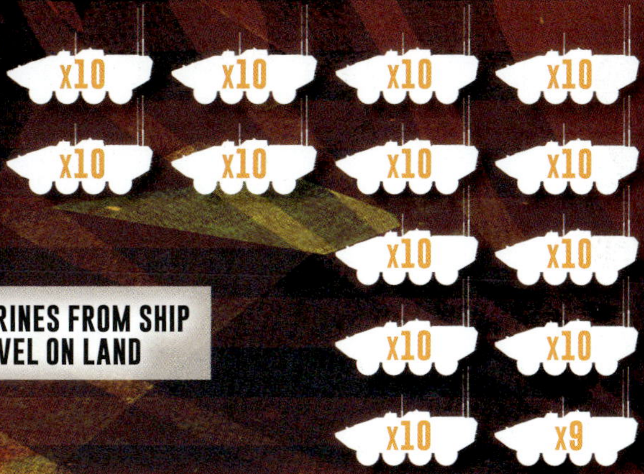

WHAT IS IT? A VEHICLE THAT MOVES MARINES FROM SHIP TO SHORE SO THEY CAN TRAVEL ON LAND

FIRST USED 2020

BODY ARMOR

Marines wear body armor vests. These vests protect them from getting badly hurt.

ARMORED COMBAT VEHICLE

Marines used **tanks** in the past. They mostly use armored combat vehicles today.

Marine aircraft support ground troops. Marines fly fighter aircraft like F-35 Lightning IIs. KC-130 Hercules are large transport airplanes. RQ-2A Pioneer **drones** help Marines see enemies.

Marines use helicopters like CH-53E Super Stallions. These move heavy equipment and supplies. Marines also use UH-1N Hueys. These carry troops and wounded Marines.

MISSIONS

Marines fought the World War II Battle of Iwo Jima in 1945. The island had an air base that would greatly help the U.S.

Marines arrived in boats. They stormed the beach. Japanese soldiers fought back with heavy fire. Marines attacked with **flamethrowers**. The bloody battle lasted weeks. Marines took control of Iwo Jima.

ARRIVAL AT IWO JIMA

MARINES NICKNAME

"Leathernecks" is the nickname for Marines. Marine uniforms used to have leather collars.

FLAMETHROWER ADVANCE

Operation Enduring Freedom began after the September 11, 2001, **terrorist** attacks. Marines flew Hornet aircraft on bombing missions to Afghanistan.

COBRA HELICOPTER

HORNET AIRCRAFT

Marines were the first U.S. ground troops in Afghanistan. They set up their Camp Rhino base at an airport. They cut off supplies in the area. Marines in Cobra helicopters attacked enemy trucks.

MISSION

OPERATION RESTORE HOPE

YEARS 1992 TO 1994

PURPOSE

MAKE A SAFE PLACE TO DROP SUPPLIES

RESULTS

MARINES HELPED GET FOOD AND MEDICINE TO PEOPLE IN SOMALIA

THE MARINE BAND

The Marine Band is called The President's Own. They play for the president.

A deadly earthquake hit Turkey in February 2023. Marines arrived in Turkey two days after the earthquake. They unloaded supplies that arrived by airplanes. They got supplies to people in need.

Marines helped build a hospital. They finished it in just five days. Doctors had a safe place to care for injured people. The U.S. Marine Corps is always ready.

MARINE CORPS PROFILE

MEMBERS TO REMEMBER

CAPTAIN VERNICE ARMOUR
The first Black female combat pilot

COLONEL JOHN GLENN
The first Marine astronaut and the first U.S. astronaut to orbit Earth

LIEUTENANT GENERAL LEWIS "CHESTY" PULLER
The most decorated Marine in Marine Corps history

MISSIONS

OPERATION RESTORE HOPE
1992

OPERATION ALLIED FORCE
1999

OPERATION IRAQI FREEDOM
2003

EMBLEM

UNITED STATES MARINE CORPS

LOGO

MARINES
THE FEW. THE PROUD.

MOTTO

"Semper Fidelis,"
Always Faithful

YEAR ESTABLISHED

1775

NUMBER OF MEMBERS

active duty in 2021

177,000

RANKS

Private First Class → General

GLOSSARY

armored combat vehicles—vehicles that move Marines around in a combat area and are protected with special coverings

bases—places where armed forces train and work

drones—aircraft that are flown by remote controls or by computers

earthquakes—events in which the earth's surface shakes; earthquakes often cause a lot of damage.

embassies—buildings where an ambassador works in a foreign country

flamethrowers—guns that shoot out burning liquid

headquarters—the main office of an organization

landslides—events in which rocks, dirt, and mud suddenly fall down a mountain

missions—jobs that Marine Corps headquarters assigns to Marines

natural disasters—natural events, such as floods, earthquakes, or hurricanes, that cause damage

Pentagon—a building in Arlington, Virginia, that is headquarters for the U.S. military

tanks—large, armored combat vehicles that move on tracks and carry weapons

terrorist—related to people who use fear to control others

TO LEARN MORE

AT THE LIBRARY

McKinney, Donna. *F-35 Lightning II.* Minneapolis, Minn.: Bellwether Media, 2024.

McKinney, Donna. *V-22 Osprey.* Minneapolis, Minn.: Bellwether Media, 2024.

Monroe, Alex. *World War II.* Minneapolis, Minn.: Bellwether Media, 2024.

ON THE WEB

FACTSURFER

Factsurfer.com gives you a safe, fun way to find more information.

1. Go to www.factsurfer.com
2. Enter "The United States Marine Corps" into the search box and click 🔍.
3. Select your book cover to see a list of related content.

INDEX

Afghanistan, 16, 17
aircraft, 5, 8, 12, 16
amphibious combat vehicle, 11
armored combat vehicles, 8, 11
bases, 6, 9, 14, 17
Battle of Iwo Jima, 14
body armor, 11
CH-53E Super Stallions, 13
Code Talkers, 8
Department of the Navy, 6
earthquakes, 4, 18
embassies, 6, 7, 9
F-35 Lightning IIs, 12
helicopters, 13, 16, 17
Japan, 4, 6
KC-130 Hercules, 12
M27 Infantry Automatic Rifles, 10
M203 Grenade Launchers, 10
Marine Band, 18
Marine Corps profile, 20–21
Marines, 5, 6, 7, 8, 9, 10, 11, 12, 13, 14, 15, 16, 17, 18, 19
missions, 6, 9, 14, 16, 17, 18, 19
MV-22 Ospreys, 5
nickname, 15
Operation Enduring Freedom, 16, 17
Operation Restore Hope, 17
peace, 9
Pentagon, 6, 7
RQ-2A Pioneer drones, 12
ships, 6
supplies, 4, 5, 13, 17, 18
troops, 8, 12, 13, 17
Turkey, 18
UH-1N Hueys, 13
wars, 8, 9
weapons, 8, 10, 14, 15
World War II, 8, 14

The images in this book are reproduced through the courtesy of: DVIDS, front cover, pp. 4, 5 (inset left, main), 7 (Marines, embassy), 8, 9 (Camp Lejeune, Camp Pendleton), 10, 11, 12 (main, inset), 13 (main, inset), 16 (main, inset), 23; DVIDS/ Wikipedia Commons, pp. 3, 9 (Air Ground Combat Center), 11 (combat vehicle); hyolee2/ Wikipedia Commons, p. 4 (inset); Xinhua/ Alamy, p. 5 (landslide); US Army Photo/ Alamy, p. 6; Jeremy Christensen, p. 7 (Pentagon); USMC Archives/ Wikipedia Commons, pp. 8 (fun fact), 14, 15 (top, middle); Marine Corps/ Wikipedia Commons, pp. 9 (Recruit Depot Parris Island, Marine Corps Base Hawaii), 10 (inset), 20 (Armour, Puller, Operation Restore Hope), 21 (emblem, logo, Private First Class, General); National Archives and Records Administration/ Wikipedia Commons, p. 15 (bottom); NB/ROD/ Alamy, p. 17 (left); US Navy/ Wikipedia Commons, p. 17 (right); Berkan4kardes, p. 18; United States Marine Band/ Wikipedia Commons, p. 18 (fun fact); Department of Defense, p. 19 (top, bottom); NASA/ Wikipedia Commons, p. 20 (Glenn); PJF Military Collection/ Alamy, p. 20 (Operation Allied Force); Pictorial Press Ltd/ Alamy, p. 20 (Operation Iraqi Freedom).